AF471381

ROSARY

Tell me

Tell me your story

Count out your tears

Count out your smiles

Tell me

Tell me everything

Be naked

For the first time in your life

TURNED

You turned me

Brought me back

I was dead

You made me alive

UNIT PRICE

How much are your tears worth?

Will you put your life into print like I did?

Are you more sad than me?

Have you had a harder time?

Will that make you more money?

It’s sad that the difference between a good or bad writer

Is how many books that people buy

CATHEDRAL ROCK

Sand

That's my memory of you
The day we shared

Sand

When I walk on the beach
Sometimes, I kneel down

Touch the sand
Brush it against my lips

Sand

Remember how it felt on your skin

REVERSE STRIPTEASE

Can't wait

To watch you

Get out of bed

Then slowly

You start to get dressed

ZOMBIE

Sometimes I think I can
Bring you back to life

Avoid your teeth and nails

Hold you close
While you try to kill me

COUNT

Count

Your

Ribs

With

Kisses

Up

Down

Then

Up

Again

JUST

You
Could be we

I
Could be us

Don't walk away
Don't think about it

Walk up to me

Just touch

SIREN

The siren cries her song

My name spelt out in tears

She calls me to the rocks

I am her prisoner

Off I sail

I stand on the deck alone

The storm terrible to behold

She smiles

I wait for her to drown me

FENCING

It's different now
But, we're always the same

Pretend we're closer
Still alone again

Situation open and transparent
Although, I'm blind to the details

We play the game
That sends me off the rails

ENEMY OF SMALL TALK

I resent people I meet
Who have not been unhappy

No issues
No tears
No scars

I resent myself because I should
Love you

But I can't

Your life is too alien by far

LOVE YOU

Love you
You know

Never told you
Never could

Talking
Not saying what I want to say

Thinking about you
Everyday

Love you

You know

CYCLES

Watch this artist at work

The special art

The art of falling apart

Watch me destroy myself

Then like a phoenix

Rise again
From the flames

Then start the whole thing going
Again and again and again

ONCE

Once

I want you to hold me so close

Breathe into my face

Tell me you cared for me

You fancied me

Loved me

Just pretend you thought about me

Once

WE

We are who we choose to be

Make decisions on what we have to feel

Advance towards the futures light

We are brave

Everything will turn out fine

TOUCH

Alone in bed
Too hot to touch

Can't touch myself
It's not enough

Won't turn around
Don't want to see

Just laying still
Pretending you're next to me

THE PICTURE OF DORIAN GRAY

Why do I say what they want to hear
Instead of what I want to say

How can I smile and joke along
While inside I cry

The veneer of me is so beautiful

Hiding the rotten corpse inside

AMAZON

I am strong in my man's way
But I could never be strong as a woman

Not last a day in a female way

I can stand violence and pain
She's seen it all before

I can love
But not understand it

be given grief
but unable to decipher it

Feel loss without the long term loss apparent

A woman can smile and love
While she's breaking down inside

A woman thinks about other people
While a man will just lay down and die

ENGAGEMENT

Watch your legs while you walk
Count your teeth when you talk

Catch the light as you smile

Look at my love for you
Reflected back at me
From your eyes

IMPERFECTION

Sometimes it’s the flaws in something

That makes it beautiful

so what’s wrong with you?

Why are you so beautiful to me?

SILENT MOVIE

Enter stage right
The hero
Pure of heart

Meet the heroine
Tied to the train tracks
She never needs to be saved

Listen to them talking

Crying over many graves

BEAUTIFUL PILLOW

To wake up
On your stomach

My cheek
Resting against your ribs

WALKAWAY

Walkaway

You always walk away

I watch you go
Don’t call to you

Walkaway

You always walk away

One day

I’ll stop running

TALK

We talk together

Everyday

Conversations
Advice
I seek your guidance

I talk to your photograph

Everyday

Enjoy the silence

NEAR DARK

I run from your gaze
With the same fear
A vampire feels
Towards the suns rays

DOUBLE SPEAK

I'm sending mixed messages

Mixed messages to you

If you can figure out

What I'm not saying

That's my message

My message

To you

FRIENDS TO THE RAIN

We're both friends to the rain

I want to hold you

Touch your face

We'll get through this

In our ways

We're both friends

Friends to the rain

MIME ARTIST

I'm clever at not saying

What I'm feeling

It's funny

The words are written all over my face

You can read them

I don't realise

ONE WORD

You can say

No

You can say

Maybe

Just don’t say

Yes

THE CHARMED ONES

We

We know

Life is hard

Has been hard

Days of beauty
Days of pain

We're here now
At this one moment

It's time to rejoice
We stand together

An invisible tattoo

That links me to you

THE FALLEN

It's not the fall
That kills you

It's having your heart
Torn out of your chest

Beforehand

NICE SENTIMENT, CRAP POEM

It's amazing how much
Love and time you put

Into writing something so beautiful
And profound

Then the next day you wake in excitement
To read what you've written

Then you realise it's terrible
And it crushes you

THE HOURS

One day

One day soon

We'll cry together

Count the Rosary

The rosary of tears

Tell of the bad days

The hours

The hours of pain

PRODIGAL SON

Feeling emotional at moment

Very sad

But actually I'm connecting with
Things I always avoid

That's a good feeling
I realise now

I'm human

Like everybody else

Hello planet

I'm glad to be home

MASCARA

Sleep

To sleep together

Under the tethered stars

Entwined

My fellow beast of burden

We’ll be covered in your mascara

When the moon releases the sun

EXODUS

Promised you one thing

I'd follow you to the end of the world

And here I am

What's my next task?
My beautiful love

www.ingramcontent.com/pod-product-compliance
Ingram Content Group UK Ltd.
Pitfield, Milton Keynes, MK11 3LW, UK
UKHW041902190726
13854UKWH00003B/1038